Leonard MacNally

Robin Hood

Or, Sherwood Forest

Leonard MacNally

Robin Hood
Or, Sherwood Forest

ISBN/EAN: 9783337069568

Printed in Europe, USA, Canada, Australia, Japan

Cover: Foto ©ninafisch / pixelio.de

More available books at **www.hansebooks.com**

ROBIN HOOD;

OR,

SHERWOOD FOREST:

A

COMIC OPERA.

AS IT IS PERFORMED AT THE

THEATRE-ROYAL,

IN

COVENT-GARDEN.

BY LEONARD MACNALLY,

The FIFTH EDITION,

WITH ALTERATIONS, AND ADDITIONS;
AS IT IS NOW PERFORMED.

———————

LONDON:

Printed by J. ALMON, at No. 182, Fleet-Street,

1787.

[Price One Shilling and Sixpence.]

DRAMATIS PERSONÆ.

MEN, Residents in the Forest.

	1784.	1787.
Robin Hood, Captain of the Outlaw Archers, — —	Mr. DAVIES.	Mr. BOWDEN.
Little John, his Friend and Bowbearer, — —	Mr. QUICK.	Mr. QUICK.
Scarlet, a principal Outlaw, —	Mr. BRETT.	Mr. BROWN.
Bowman, another Outlaw,	Mr. CUBIT.	Mr. CUBIT.
Outlaws and Archers, —	{ Mr. DARLEY. Mr. DOYLE	Mr. DARLEY. Mr. DOYLE.
Allen-a-Dale, the Shepherd of the Forest, — —	Mrs. KENNEDY.	Mrs. KENNEDY.

MEN, Visitors to the Forest.

Ruttekin, an itinerant Tinker,	Mr. EDWIN.	Mr. EDWIN.
Baron Fitzherbert, disguised a Friar Tuck, — —	Mr. WILSON.	Mr. BOOTH.
Edwin, the Hermit of the Dale,	Mr. JOHNSTONE.	Mr. JOHNSTONE.

WOMAN, Resident in the Forest.

Stella, a Shepherdess,	Miss WHEELER.	Mrs. WELLS.

WOMEN, not Resident in the Forest.

Clorinda, Huntress of Titbury,	Mrs. MARTYR.	Mrs. MARTYR.
Annette, the tiny Foot Page,	Mrs. WILSON.	Mrs. BROWN.
Angelina, a Pilgrim, —	Mrs. BANNISTER.	Mrs. BILLINGTON.

The SCENE lies in Sherwood Forest.

A

ROBIN HOOD;

OR,

SHERWOOD FOREST.

ACT I.

Scene a deep wood terminating in visto—Several cots shaded by trees: on one side of the stage, Archers making arrows: on the other side, Stella and other women with distaffs, sitting at their several doors.

GLEE.

IN Sherwood's grove,
  The sweets of love,
We'll taste and drink till we're mellow;
  With dimpled smiles,
  Sly winks and wiles,
Each lass will please her fellow.
    Ranting,
    Flanting,
  Gay gallanting,
Such sports the like ne'er seen O !
  Hey down derry, derry,
  Merry maids and archers,
Tripping it on the green O.——

Bowman. Here comes Little John.——

Enter JOHN, *carrying a large bow.*

John. Well sung and strongly, my blithe lads and hearty lasses—like true out-laws who lighten the heavy purses of the rich with clear consciences, share your

         B   booty

booty with the poor, and wash down repentance with cups of nappy brown ale.

Stella. Girls let us retire.

⌊*The women retire into the cots.*

Bowman. Why are we called out-laws, John?

John. I'll tell you. Laws were made to punish rogues; but we being honest fellows, are put out of the law.

Bowman. Then honesty and law are not found together.

John. True, and therefore being honest we live against the law; and yet, with due deference to the learned profession, we live honestly as those who live by the law.

Bowman. Right, John.

John. Mark—We kill the King's deer, and are called thieves; but who are the greatest thieves, we who feed on royal venison, or those who prey upon his Majesty's liege subjects? Stand close and attend to me lads—our captain, the brave Earl of Huntingdon, has a call upon our service, therefore every man must look to his arms; let your quivers be well stockt with arrows, and see that your bow-strings are all found. This night we sally forth on an expedition.

Bowman. What is the cause?

John. Our Captain you all know was betrothed to the fair Clorinda, niece to Baron Fitz Herbert. You also know, that on the very eve of marriage he was ordered from court.

Bowman. True.

John. Now this was all owing to the Bishop of Hereford, who maliciously poisoned the royal ear, and the instant the noble Huntingdon became an object of the King's displeasure, the whole court tribe, even the very caterpillars who fed upon his bounty avoided him as if he was contagious.

Bowman. But we, John, stuck to him and will while we have life.

John. Give me your hand—a man never truly knows his friends till misfortune overtakes him. But mark—

Our

Our leader's heart is fixed upon the Lady Clorinda, and she loves him with equal ardour; but the proud Baron, her uncle, keeps her locked up, and prevents all intercourse between them.

Bowman. Why not attack the Baron's castle and carry her off by force———

John. That is the business you are to be employed on—we will execute it this very night; but not a word to Robin; voluntary service is most valuable, and to-morrow, I trust, we shall be able to present his mistress to him—(*A horn sounds*)—Hark! Scarlet's horn.

Enter SCARLET, *and Archers, with* RUTTEKIN *the Tin-ker, prisoner; an Archer carrying his budget.*

John. Brave Scarlet, welcome!—Who have we got here? (*Examining Ruttekin.*)

Scarlet. We discovered a company of men, within the purlieus of the Forest, on their way we suppose to the assizes at Nottingham.

John. On their way to the assizes! O the unconscionable dogs! with intent no doubt to sue their honest debtors.

Scarlet. They fled, and all escaped but this fellow.

John. What are you, sirrah?

Ruttekin. A tinker and a fool, but no knave.

John. Well distinguished; for though all knaves are fools, all fools are not knaves. Where do you reside tinker?

Ruttekin. Where I stand. I carry my shop on my back, as the snail carries his house; am always at home, yet am a traveller.

John. A fool a traveller; but that is no new case, many of our travellers having proved themselves fool. Let the tinker be free. But say, lads, what plunder have you brought in?

Scarlet. Not much. We met a monk, who denied having cash, but Robin forced him to pray to his titular saint for some, and after five minutes devotion, on searching his reverence, we found twenty broad pieces in his hood; but the money did not remain long with us: falling in with one of the bishop of Hereford's tenants, who was flying from his habitation, being unable to pay his rent, Robin, with his accustomed humanity made him a present of the friar's tribute.

John. Perhaps this fellow is an impostor, so open his pack *(pointing to* Ruttekin): A good heart may lie in a deformed body; a diamond may be concealed in a dunghill, and why not gold or silver in this budget. [*They open the budget and throw out a fowl. a bottle, and a loaf;* Ruttekin *leaps into it.*]

Ruttekin. Spare my property! my budget contains my ways and means!

Scarlet. Out of the budget, or I'll knock you down.

Ruttekin. What, strike a man in his own shop?

(*Horn sounds.*

John. There goes Robin's blast and calls me—Away lads; reinstate master Tinker in possession of his shop and moveables, and give the poor devil some refreshment.

Ruttekin.. Lead away, my ferry folk, and I'll dance after you.

A I R.

I mend pottles and canns,
Hoop juggs, patch kettles and pans,
   And over the country trudge it;
I sing without measure,
Nor fear loss of treasure,
   And carry my all in my budget.

Here under the green leav'd bushes,
   Oh how we'll firk it,
   Caper and jirk it,
Singing as blithe as thrushes,

I'm not plagued with a wife,
Live free from contest and strife,
   Blow high, blow low——Ruttekin never
    minds it.

I eat

I eat when I'm hungry,
Drink when I'm dry,
    Join pleasure wherever I find it.

Here under the green leav'd bushes,
    Oh how we'll firk it,
    Caper and jirk it,
Singing as blithe as thrushes.   [*Exeunt.*

Enter FRIAR *and* JOHN, *fighting with quarter-staves, two*
ARCHERS *following.*

1st Archer. Well done, John!

2d Archer. Well laid on, Friar!

John. Let no man strike who loves me. Friar, you
have beaten me soundly; I retain the music of your
fiddle-stick in both my ears.—O heaven preserve us
from the heavy arm of Mother Church!

Friar. Have I done you justice?

John. Yes, justice with a vengeance!—To give the
devil his due, this infernal divine fights with Christian
fortitude.—The last blow staggered my conscience.—
But will you live among us, priest?

Friar. With all my heart, upon this condition, that
if you need a chaplain, I may serve you and your friends
in that capacity.

John. Will you be true?

Friar. To the last moment I will be true to you—
will attend to shrive little Little John, even at the
gallows.

John. I thank your charity, reverend Sir; and as one
good turn deserves another, be assured you shall not
want a friend to shake hands with at the gibbet. Our
chaplain you shall be; a confessor, my hearts, will
make us new men every day; by absolving us in the
morning for our trespasses over-night.—But we must
not have too much devotion.

Friar. Never fear—Though I wear the habit of the
church, I am no devotee; I love my friends, pray for
my enemies, and my principal study is the art of living
well with all mankind.

John.

John. And women-kind I prefume——

Friar. Who ordained you a confeffor ?—But in truth, though I have taken the vow of celibacy, I reprobate a fingle life among the laity, and think that were the fuperfluous productions of nature to be pruned away, the bufinefs fhould commence by lopping off old maids and fufty batchelors.

John. Right—they are a malignant generation, and, like the rattlefnake, increafe in noife and venom with their years. To what monaftery do you belong?

Friar. To none; I am juft arrived from a crufade.

John. I thought fo, for you laid on like a Turk.

Enter BOWMAN, *with a fheathed Sword.*

Bowman. A ftranger has furrendered to one of our out-pofts, and is coming this way. He demands an audience with Robin Hood immediately, and fends his fword.   [*Delivers his fword to* John.

John. Conduct the ftranger before us—and fee, Mafter Bowman, take care of this honeft Friar; let him have liquor to moiften the clay, for I fee by his ruby nofe, he is a wet foul with a dry liver.

Friar. Go on, my lad; and remember your orders —let me have liquor plenty to moiften the clay.——

A I R.

When the chill fciroco blows,
　　And winter tells a heavy tale;
When pies, and daws, and rooks, and crows,
Do fit and curfe the froft and fnows;
　　　Then give me ale,
　　　Old brown ale,
　　　Nut brown ale,
　　　Stout brown ale.

O give me ftout brown ale——
Ale that the plowman's heart up keeps,
　　And equals it to tyrant thrones;
That wipes the eye that ever weeps,
　　And lulls in fweet and dainty fleeps
　　　Th' o'er wearied bones——
　　　Old brown ale, &c.

John.

John. Well chaunted, and merrily; a goodly pfalm-finger; yet his notes would found better in a tavern than a cathedral.

Enter EDWIN, *guarded.*

Edwin. I have told you my bufinefs is with Robin Hood only   *(To the guard.*

John. That may be, but you cannot fee the great Robin, till firft examined by Little John. Who are you, Sir?

Edwin. A *Gentleman,* courteous Sir, who wifhes to be confidered *your* humble fervant.

John. Fairly fpoken—An humble fervant is good, becaufe it is a rarity, moft fervants affuming more impudence than their mafters. Now *Gentleman* is bad, though it is a good title to travel with, or live by; for every fellow, who has neither property nor profeffion, and is too lazy to work, begs or plunders under the character of a *Gentleman.*

Edwin. I agree with you, Sir; and the country is over-run with fuch vermin.

John. Here comes our leader——

Enter Robin.

Noble Captain, this gentleman, who fays he is my humble fervant, defires to fpeak with you.

Robin. I like his prefence.——You appear a foldier, Sir.——Return him his fword. *(To John)* It is my way to meet every man on equal terms; and if you come for a trial of fkill, my bow-bearer will fee fair play.

John. Never doubt my honour; and if you beat Robin to-day, John will indulge you with a bout to-morrow.

Edwin. I would fpeak in private.

John. Then I withdraw; and, in truth, I am not in good fighting order—Stella has run away with my heart; and this Friar has raifed fo many knobs on my head, it feels like a bunch of grapes.   *[Exit.*

Robin. Now, Sir, what are your commands?

                       Edwin.

Edwin. Courage and generofity are congenial qualities : I am confident you poffefs the firft, and doubt
not but I fhall experience the latter.

Robin. You fpeak from a brave and candid foul.
Whatever my men have taken fhall be returned.

Edwin. I only wifh them to reftore a hermit's gar-
ment. You fee before you an unhappy man, fcorned
by the woman he loves, urged by defpair, yet doating
on the caufe of his mifery. O heaven! is there no
comfort for me?

A I R.

Ye pow'rs who make virtue your care,
   O bend from your bowers above;
Say, why fhould diftrefs and defpair
   Be the conftant attendants on love?

Should war with its wide fpreading force,
   Of nations the fcourge and the curfe,
To ten-fold its rage be encreas'd,
   The torments of lovers are worfe.

Ye power's who make virtue your care,
   O bend from your bowers above;
Say, why fhould diftrefs and defpair
   Be the conftant attendants on love?

Robin. Your forrows breathing the genuine feelings
of an injured mind, engage my friendfhip. Is it your
intention to join our party? You may command here
every thing conducive to your eafe.

Edwin. You have my thanks, but I muft refufe your
generous offer. My mind, long labouring with grief,
has determined upon retirement: underftanding there
is a hermitage in the Foreft, lately occupied by a holy
man, now dead there, and loft to the world, I wifh to
become his melancholy fucceffor, and pine out a life of
wretchednefs.

Robin. May I enquire who you are?

Edwin. My name is Edwin, fon to Sir Launcelot
Barnard; I am juft arrived from Paleftine, where for
three

three years ferving under a borrowed name, I fought for death in battle.

Robin. Command my fervices. I knew your father well, and often under him repelled my country's foes. The ingratitude of thofe I loved and ferved has driven me into this Foreft, an outlaw—but no more of that—Though rough in manners, and poffeffing afperity againft the proud, the avaricious, and the luxuriant, you fhall find me not ungenerous to the diftreffed.

Edwin. 'Tis to your generofity I apply; the fimplicity of your manners I admire, and defpife the fuperficial civilities of life; the mind of a foldier, like his fword, is more valuable for its temper than its polifh.

Robin. Henceforward we are friends; but come let us in and drink a pledge to future amity. Edwin, your hand (*takes Edwin's hand*) I feel for you. Alas! I am myfelf a lover, and though belov'd in return, fuffer under all the excruciating pangs of abfence.

DUET.

The ftag through the Foreft when rous'd by the horn,
Sore frighted, high bounding, flies wretched, forlorn;
Quick panting, heart burfting, the hounds now in view,
Speed doubles, fpeed doubles, they eager purfue.
But 'fcaping the hunters, again through the groves.
Forgetting paft evils, with freedom he roves.
Not fo in his foul, who from tyrant love flies,
The fhaft ftill remains, and defpairing he dies.
[*Exeunt.*

Enter ALLEN *and* STELLA.

Allen. I am certain fomething diftreffes you, tell me my dear fifter, what it is? I your brother and friend,

have

have a right to queſtion you: believe me, Stella, few women would fall into error, if they made confidants of their male relations.

Stella. I do believe you love me, brother; and I hope you have no reaſon to complain of my wanting affection. Let me aſk you a queſtion; what think you of Will Scarlet?

Allen. That, in manners, he is a vain fop; and in his heart a cunning deceiver. Like an overripe pear, fair without, but bad within.

Stella. You are right, brother, he is a fop; for when he brings home poſies from the meadows, he always culls the ſweeteſt and prettieſt to ornament himſelf! and he is a deceiver, as poor Martha knows to her coſt. Oh! poor Martha! ſhe was once the very life of the Foreſt.

A I R.

" The laughing pow'rs
" That led the wanton hours,
" When May was in her prime,
" Open'd the cells of flow'rs
" To airy paramours.
" And bid the love-ſick poet ſigh in rhyme."

Oh! ſummer all too fair;
Oh! bliſſes all too high!
Oh! might ſhe not have known,
That ſweeteſt flow'r, the ſooneſt blown,
Is ſooneſt gone—
That cleareſt ſtream beneath a ſummer ſky
May ſoon be dry!

She never ſaid,
Can my dear love fly,
Till he was fled!

But what think you of Little John?

Allen. I think him a ruſſetan, a goodly apple, with a plain outſide, but ſound core.

Stella

Stella. And I think fo too; for he ſtrews thyme under my window, when he thinks I do not fee him; and when he gathers wild ſtrawberries, or filberts, or finds honeycombs in the woods, he always preſents them to me untouched.

Allen. There is as much difference between John and Scarlet, as between an honeſt man and a knave. I know they are both your admirers, but be cautious in beſtowing your affection; you are very young, Stella; and love, my girl, has its bitters as well as its ſweets.

Stella. I would tell you a fecret—but you muſt hear me without cenſure; or if you reprove, remember the leſſons of affection make the deepeſt impreſſions when breathed in gentleneſs.

Allen. Speak with freedom. Something I fear has hurt you.

Stella. Yes, I am hurt, yet I cannot tell where. I am pleaſed too, yet I cannot tell why. I ſigh when I wiſh to ſmile. Nay more, I am warm in the cool ſhade, and freeze even in the ſun. Heigh ho!

Allen. And how long have you had this complaint?

Stella. How long! It has been coming on me by degrees at leaſt theſe long, long two months. Let me whiſper you a queſtion; nay, turn your head, I cannot ſpeak while you look me in the face. You muſt know, Little John this day gave me ſome wild plumbs—La, I cannot ſay a word more!

Allen. Then the complaint lies there.

Stella. Where, brother, where?—mercy, ſhew me! Sure I do not eat too many wild plumbs—where does the complaint lie? I feel the pain, but cannot diſcover the ſeat of it.

Allen. Lay your hand upon your heart and pronounce the name of John.

Stella. There—John, John, John—Bleſs me! how it beats—pit, pit, pit, pat—Heigh ho! my complaint I find is the heart-burn and palpitation.

Allen. The truth is you love John.

Stella. Love a man! O fie! Yet, certainly I have a great friendſhip for John. You know, brother, when

I fell into the river, he plunged in and saved my life, while Scarlet run for affiftance.

Allen. I do not blame your gratitude ; but be cautious, John's fimplicity might prove as injurious as Scarlet's cunning.

Stella. I'll follow your advice, for I have heard young girls often meet with ruin where they expect fecurity—

Allen. And ever after fuffer under the pangs of fhame, repentance, and bitter grief.

A I R.

Hard beats her heart, her eyes pour tears,.
Corroding grief confumes her years ;
No more fhe fports with damfels gay,
But mourns in penance night and day.
Love makes her happy for a while,
And then, like thee, fhe'll chearful fmile ;
But foon the willow binds her head—
She mourns a lover from her fled,

[*Exeunt.*

Scene changes to another part of the foreft. Enter CLO-RINDA *in the drefs of a huntrefs, with bow and quiver ;* ANGELINA *as a male pilgrim ;* ANNETTE *as her page.*

Clorinda. Nay, let me perfuade you, my fweet coufin, do not depart till you fee the refult of my adventure.

Angelina. That is impoffible, my vow prohibits me : I will not reft till I have reached the coaft, nor will I return till I meet tidings of my love.

Clorinda. But we are now near the bower of my lover—O Cupid ! thou tyrant of the paffions, be merciful to thy poor petitioner.

Well, this love has fet you both mad ; but your madnefs, Madam, (*to Clorinda*) a think the moft defirable. Heaven defend me from the afflictions of my lady, my lord a mean ! Melancholy madnefs is horrible ! But let who will figh, I will laugh through life while I breathe. La ! I have had lovers of all
pro-

professions, and played them off with equal indiffe-
rence.

A I R.

When the men a courting came,
　Flattering with their prittle prattle;
Of their fool'ries I made game,
　Rally'd with my tittle tattle.
　　　　Cooing to me,
　　　　Woeing to me,
　　　　Teasing of me,
　　　　Pleasing of me,
　　　　Off'ring pelf,
　　　　Each silly elf
Came wooing, cooing, bowing to me.

The learn'd serjeant of the law
　Shew'd his parchments, briefs, and papers;
In his deeds I found a flaw,
　So dismiss'd him in the vapours.
　　　　Cooing to me,
　　　　Wooing to me,
　　　　Teasing of me,
　　　　Pleasing of me,
　　　　Off'ring pelf,
　　　　Each silly elf
Came wooing, cooing, bowing to me.

Physic old display'd his wealth,
　With his nostrums, but the fact is,
I swore loud I'd keep my health,
　Nor die martyr to his practice.
　　　　Cooing to me,
　　　　Wooing to me,
　　　　Teasing of me,
　　　　Pleasing of me,
　　　　Off'ring pelf,
　　　　Each silly elf
Came wooing, cooing, bowing to me.

But

But at laſt a Swain bow'd low,
  Candid, handſome, tall, and clever,
Squeez'd my hand, I can't tell how,
  But he won my heart for ever.
      Cooing to me,
      Wooing to me,
      Preſſing of me,
      Bleſſing of me,
      He's no pelf,
      Yet for himſelf
I'll ſend all other lovers from me.

Angelina. Some one comes this way.

Clorinda. One of the merry archers—Hillo! hillo! tantivy!

John. (*within*) Hillo! hillo! hilloa!

Enter JOHN.

By St. Dunſtan's ſhrine a Diana! and with a voice ſhrill as a lark! Egad, fair nymph, you make the welk'n ring with your ſhrill notes. But why ſalute me with a tantivy; I being a batchellor, and that congratulation only due to married gentry, who come under the deſcription of bucks? (*to* Clorinda. Save your reverence, (*bowing to* Angelina) I preſume you are a palmer, performing penance for the ſins of your fathers, for thou art too young to have tranſgreſſed thyſelf. But may I enquire, are you returning from, or going on a pilgrimage?

Annette. Why aſk? what is your reaſon? and what right has my maſter to anſwer you?

John. Here is a chatterer! Pray, my little magpie, has your tongue been ſplit with a ſilver groat, that it wags ſo glibly?

Annette. You muſt know, my good friend, I and my maſter have traverſed France, croſſed the Alps, viſited Jeruſalem, made an excurſion into Turkey, and——

John. Enough, enough—Egad, my lad of wax, the hinges of your tongue want no oiling. But pray now,

to

to what purpose did you go throug chall this fa-
tigue?

Annette. In truth, to little purpose: our objects
were beauty and virtue, both of which we find flourish
better at home than in any other soil. Pray, Sir,
give this inquisitive fellow an account of your travels.

Angelina. I wil indulge him with all my heart, and
then, fair coulin, without any further ceremony, or
even a farewel, I shall depart (*to* Clarinda.) My page
has told you beauty and virtue were the objects of my
search.

B A L L A D.

I travers'd Judah's barren sand,
    At Beauty's altar to adore;
But there the Turk had spoil'd the land,
    And Sion's daughters were no more.

In Greece the bold imperious mein,
    The wanton look, the leering eye,
Bade Love's devotion not be seen,
    Where constancy is never nigh.

From thence to Italy's fair shore,
    I urg'd my never ceasing way,
And to Loretta's temple bore
    A mind devoted still to pray.

But there too Superstition's hand
    Had sickly'd every feature o'er,
And made me soon regain the land,
    Where beauty fills the western shore;

Where Hymen with Cœlestial power
    Connubial transport doth adorn,
Where purest virtue sports the hour,
    That ushers in each happy morn.

Ye daughters of old Albion's Isle,
    Where'er I go, where'er I strav,
O, Charity's sweet children, smile,
    To cheer a Pilgrim on his way!

Clorinda

Clorinda. May cheerfulncfs be thy guide, and fafety thy attendant.

                     [*Exeunt* Angelina *and* Annette.

John. I fay Amen, from the depth of my heart. And now, you more than mortal, what is your bufinefs in the Foreft ?

Clorinda. I feek a known bold archer, who draws his bow with fkill, and can pierce an aple, or fplit a wand at threefcore yards diftance.

John. Then you have hit the mark ; and though I fay it, who fhould not fay it, there is not a tighter fellow of his inches in the Foreft, than your humble fervant, Little John.

Clorinda. Art thou Little John ?

John. The fame lady—But fee, I have no apprehenfion from the quiver of your eyes ; my affections are engaged, and my heart is proof againft their arrows. But for your comfort, there are charitable men enough in the Foreft, and you may fecure half a dozen ftrings to your bow.

Clorinda. Half a dozen! cry you, mercy Little John ; I have heard of your prowefs, it is true, but feek a man at leaft a foot taller.

A I R.

The tramp of fame your name has breath'd,
    Its praife has founded far and near ;
Stout Little John, with laurel wreath'd,
    Hath reach'd each dame and damfel's ear.
But 'tis not you ; bold Robin Hood
I come to feek with bended bow,
       That man of might
       I fain would fight,
And conquer with my oh, ho, oh !
     Through froft and fnow,
     Though cold winds blow
     I never fail,
     In rain or hail,
     Though thunders roll
     From pole to pole,
To conquer with my oh, ho, ho !

                                     With

With bended bow,
The buck or doe,
I never fail,
Through rain or hail,
Though thunders roll
From pole to pole,
To conquer with my oh, ho, ho!

John. 'Fore George, damfel, you fing a merry ftave; but Robin will never fight you, fo there is comfort for you and your oh, ho, ho!—But here he comes, and with him a poor love-fick devil, going to turn hermit——

Clorinda. It is, indeed, my dear Robin.

John. Dear Robin! Who are you? Speak nymph, I begin to fufpect——

Clorinda. Step afide and I will tell you.

John. Your lily hand; *(takes her hand)* for egad, damfel, I like you and your oh, ho, ho!

[*Exeunt.*

Enter ROBIN *and* EDWIN.

Robin. It grieves me, I cannot pefuade you to remain with us; time and reflection, with cheerful company and the fports of the chace, would alleviate your pain.

Edwin. No, no—I have tried every means in vain: three years abfence has not leffened, but encreafed my paffion and my grief—even hope, that fweet'ning balm which attends the martyred wretch ftrained on the rack in his laft pangs of torture, is denied to me.

Robin. Pray hear me.

Edwin. Do not urge me—my life I have devoted to heaven, and will perfevere——permit one of your archers to conduct me to the hermitage.

Robin. You fhall be obliged; and yet I hope for your affiftance and advice in recovering my love, my dear Clorinda!

Edwin. You fhall have my prayers—fuccefs attend your efforts. You venture for a woman who recipro-

D cates

crates your paffion, and will reward it; I fuffer for an unfeeling maid, whofe fcorn was inftant death, did not her beauty falve the wound it gives.

A I R.

Her hair is l'ke a golden clue,
    Drawn from Minerva's loom ;
Her lips carnations dropping dew,
    Her breath is a perfume.

Her brow is like the mountain fnow,
    Gilt by the morning beam :
Her cheeks like living rofes blow,
    Her eyes like azure ftream.

Adieu, my friend, be me forgot,
    And from thy mind defac'd ;
But may that happinefs be thine,
    Which I can never tafte.   [*Exit.*

Enter JOHN.

John. Clear the clouds from your brow, and pre-pare for laughter ; I have a merry tale to tickle your fancy with.

Robin. Poftpone your merriment, good John : I am in a melancholy mood, and would indulge it.

John. I bring fomething to rouze your fpirits—A challenge, and there lies the gauntlet.

Robin. A woman's glove.   (*Takes up the glove.*

John. I know not whether man or woman ; but the challenger is here in the Foreft, and fwears to beat you with an Oh, ho, ho !   [*Exit.*

Robin. Perhaps fome lover of my Clorinda ! here comes the ftranger.

Enter JOHN, *leading* CLORINDA, *her head turned from* R O B I N.

Robin. A woman !

                              John.

John. I fay a goddefs—but turn your head this way, pleafe your goddefsfhip; for if you fight here it muft be face to face.

Clorinda. (*Looking towards* Robin.) Not know me, Robin!

Robin. It is Clorinda, my life, my love! [*Embrace.*

John. Egad that is a Cornifh hug!

Clorinda. O Robin—I have ventured all for you! will you not think lightly of me? am I not leffened in your efteem, for thus boldly ftepping beyond the bounds prefcribed my fex?

Robin. Say, how haft thou efcaped?—I had refolved as foon as too-morrow's fun fet from the world, to force you from your tyrant.

John. Then you had been difappointed, for I had refolved with the affiftance of Allen-a-Dale, and our merry men to have done the bufinefs this very night unknown to you. It is a great difappointment to me, fair lady, to be deprived the pleafure of knocking the old proud Baron, your Uncle, on the head.

Clorinda. My uncle went yefterday to court, in confequence of an order from the king; and it is rumoured the French have threatened an invafion. I availed myfelf of his abfence, and fled to you, my love.

Robin. To live in this dreary Foreft; but it is not dreary—where you refide the fweeteft violets blow—fpring fports around your walks; and when you fmile, the coldeft hearts rejoice with fummer's warmth.

A I R.

Charming Clorinda! ev'ry note
   You breathe thefe woods among
   Shall move my grateful tongue,
Swelling my ardent throat,
   Homage devout to pay,
   Love harmonize the lay,
     And footh her with the fong!

Should

Should fhe, bewilder'd, chance to ftray,
 Ye fongfters, near your groves,
  To her your notes belong ;
 My foul its fenfe fhall prove,
 My voice its powers difplay,
 Love harmonize the lay,
  And footh her with the fong !

John. See the merry archers returning from the chace.

   Enter STELLA, SCARLET, ALLEN, *&c.*

Robin. My friends, congratulate me : I have reco-
vered my Clorinda, and we will have a jovial day.
Love has found his way into the Foreft, and to refufe
him an hofpitable reception, would be ungrateful.

 John. Stella, why filent? Lady, this is the tender
dove of my affection, and you fhall folicit for me : (*To
Clorinda*) But let's into the bower—Old Splice'em the
friar, who arrived this morning, came in pudding-time,
and if I can prevail on Stella, he fhall fhortly lug out
his horn-book.

G L E E.

 By dark grove, fhade, or winding dell,
 We merry maids and archers dwell ;
 In quiet here, from worldly ftrife,
 We pafs a cheerful rural life ;
And by the Moon's pale quivering beams,
We frifk it near the chryftal ftreams.

 Our ftation's on the king's high-way,
 We rob the rich the poor to pay :
 The woe-worn wretch we ftill protect,
 The widow, orphan ne'er neglect :
Fat churchmen proud we caufe to ftand,
And whiftle for our fteady band.

         A C T

A C T II.

Scene, *the outside of* Allen's *cot; a view of sheep feed-
ing at a distance; a bench at the door;* Allen *and*
Stella *discovered sitting.*

A L L E N.

I THANK you, my dear sister, for your attention to
my advice: but I must to my flocks; farewel, and
ever remember this, my dear girl, that though female
virtue is an inestimable diamond, it is delicacy which
gives it polish and brilliancy of the first water.

Stella. I shall remember your instructions.

D U E T.

A L L E N.

The vi'let nurs'd in woodland wild,
Young Zephyr's bride, Spring's first-born child,
　　Whose vest in heaven's tint is dy'd;
How fade it's beauties on the sight,
No more its perfume yields delight,
　　When the rich rose unfolds its pride!

S T E L L A.

The feather'd tribes, who in the groves
With shrills mellifluous woo their loves,
　　As Nature's self inspires the strain;
Their melting music fails to please,
Harsh and untuneful are their lays,
　　When Philomel awakes the plain.

B O T H.

The maid endow'd with virtue's grace,
Appears with soul-subduing face,

And

And fhines in beauty's fphere fupreme;
Each nymph that won the heart before,
By her eclips'd, can charm no more,
And all her fov'reign pow'r proclaim!

[*Exit* Allen.

Stella. Here comes my butterfly lover : he fquints his eye at me, though I am fure he admires his own face more than mine, or he would not fo often peep into the brook. He walks this way, fo I will ftop and play the rogue with him.—Blefs me ! where can it be ? (*Searching her pockets*) It muft have been fomewhere hereabouts. (*Looks round*) I would not have loft it for ———

Enter SCARLET.

Scarlet. What have you loft, my pretty Stella ?

Stella. How cou'd you frighten me by coming fo fuddenly ? I have loft—La ! you cannot think what I have loft. ———

Scarlet. And I have loft——What do you think I have loft ?

Stella. Not your fenfes, I hope ?

Scarlet. Why, in truth, even them ; a man who has loft his heart, generally lofes his fenfes.

Stella. Loft your heart ! Why carry it fo loofe in your breaft ? But fome filly girl will pick it up, and return it ; fo farewel, thou heartlefs man.   [*Going.*

Scarlet. Why fly me ?

Stella. Becaufe I fear you.

Scarlet. And why fear me ?

Stella. Becaufe you are a man, and, by your own confeffion, a heartlefs man ; now, a man without a heart fhould always be avoided by a woman.

Scarlet. Stella, I love you.

Stella. So do I, moft fincerely.

Scarlet. What, my charmer ?

Stella. Love myfelf to be fure.

Scarlet. Be ferious : few men in the Foreft can boaft better pretenfions to a maiden's regard than myfelf, and you may lofe me. Hear me, my fweet girl.

A I R.

AIR.

I love you by Heaven, what can I say more?
   Then set not my passion a cooling;
If thou yield'st not at once, I must e'en give thee
   o'er,
   For I'm but a novice at fooling.

What my love wants in words, it shall make up in
   deeds,
   Then why should we waste time in stuff, child?
A performance, you know well, a promise exceeds,
   And a word to the wife is enough, child.

Stella. But I am such a fool I shall not take your
hints; so farewell.

Scarlet. One word.——

 Stella. Yes.——   [*Running off, he stops her.*

Scarlet. Yes—that is one word indeed; but you must
not go.

Enter RUTTEKIN.

Ruttekin. No, you must not go.

Scarlet. Devil take this fool.

Stella. Why curse the fool, without including the
knave? He is the worst character of the two.

Ruttek. My budget and tools against your doublet,
I know what you are about.

Scarlet. Are you a gambler?

Ruttek. You say I am a fool; and did you ever know
a gambler who was not a fool, unless he was a rogue?
They are all either pigeons or rooks.

Stella. Well, I am gone.

Scarlet. And I follow.

Stella. By these hands you shall not.   [*Exit.*

Scarlet. By these legs I will.   [*Exit.*

Ruttek. Ha, ha, ha! Well run doe! well run buck!
But, ha! by the Mass the buck has fallen into a toil.

Enter JOHN *and* SCARLET.

John. I say, Scarlet, I am angry.

Scarlet. Angry! No, no; you are jealous, John, jealous.

John. Jealous! It is false. Except among such jack-a-dandies as you, jealousy is not of this country's growth; nor indeed of any country where the people can lay claim to manhood. I am angry.

Scarlet. I was never better pleased in my life: the smiles of a fine girl have raised my spirits.

John. But you must resign all pretensions to that fine girl, my fripperary jay. She can have but one of us, and you are not the man.

Scarlet. You must resign all pretensions to that fine girl, my rustic clown. She can have but one of us, and I am the man.

Ruttek. Let me decide this dispute. What are your pretensions?

Scarlet. I love her.

Ruttek. You love her.——What do you say?

John. I love her.

Ruttek You love her too.—So far your claims are equal. What would you do for her?

Scarlet. Die for her?

John. Then die and be —— (*whistles*). I live for her, and her alone.

Ruttek. You would die for her, (*to* Scarlet). You would live for her, (*to* John). John, you are the man; for any woman, be she ever so young, or ever so foolish, would prefer one living lover to a whole church-yard full of dead ones.

John. See, Scarlet, we are both fond of the girl: I would make her my wife, but your designs are knavish. Your false-heartedness to girls is notorious; it rises with the morning lark, and preys nightly with the owl.

Scarlet. And what then?

John.

John. Mark my words—if you dare attempt any villainy againſt the chaſtity of Stella, may I never draw an arrow to the head, if I don't ſplit you from the coxcomb to the waiſtband.

Scarlet. Ha ha, ha!

John. Yes, and hang up your perfumed carcaſe on one of thoſe trees, to whiſtle and ſwing in the wind, like the ſign of the Spread Eagle.

Ruttek. What! promote him to the office of ſcare-crow, to frighten rooks from the Foreſt?

Scarlet. If you are for that work, let us determine the conteſt this inſtant. (*Draws his ſword.*)

Ruttek. (*Holding* John.) Don't ſplit him while I am here!

John. Let me at him, Tinker: Yet it kicks againſt the grain of my manhood to ſtain my ſword with ſplit-ting a ſpliced plover; a fellow who ſmells ſavory as a jack with a pudding in its belly; who plaiſters his face over-night with greaſe and flour, and looks in the morning, for all the world, like a pigeon in paſte.

Ruttek. Take a fool's advice in this buſineſs; court the girl openly, and let him who wins her, wear her.

Scarlet. There is wiſdom in the fool's advice.

John. And I agree to the fool's advice; he is a wiſe fool.

Ruttek. Right, lads! Riſk your lives for a woman! Ha, ha, ha! What woman would do ſo for you, my dapper jack-aſſes, pigmies of fourteen to the dozen! It is more than I could expect, who am a man of ſize: but I never quarrel for my miſtreſſes, though always ſouſed over head and ears in the tender paſſion; ena-moured with every landlady and tapſtreſs over the country, the Soldan of Perſia is not a greater Turk at the buſineſs.

A I R.

Margarita firſt poſſeſt,
I remember well, my breaſt,
  With her row de dow dow de dow dow
   derrow.

    E   With

With my reftlefs heart next play'd
Martha, buxom floe-ey'd maid,
   With her tantarara row.

She to Katharine gave place;
Kate, to Betfy's am'rous face,
   With, &c.

Mary then, and gentle Ann,
Both to reign at once began,
   With their, &c.

Jenny next, a tyrant fhe,
But Rebecca fet me free,
   With my, &c.

In a week from her I fled,
And took Judith in her ftead,
   With my, &c.

She poffefs'd a wond'rous grace,
But fhe wanted Sufan's face,
   With my, &c.

Ifabella's rolling eye,
Eclipfed Sufan's prefently,
   With her, &c.

Brown-fkinn'd Befs I next obey'd,
Then lov'd Nanny, red-hair'd maid,
   With my, &c.

None could bind me, I am free,
Yet love all the fair I fee,
   With my tantarara row.

   With my row de dow dow de dow dow
     derrow,
    Tantarara row.   *[Exeunt.*

Enter

Enter FRIAR *and* CLORINDA.

Friar. Well niece, I see you are surprized.

Clorinda. Surprized! I am astonished, frighted to death.

Friar. Niece, niece, thou art the wildest doe in the Forest; thou hast over-leaped the pale of prudence, and delicacy, and art a very outlaw—O, I blush at this transgression of duty and modesty!

Clorinda. You mean my emancipation from tyranny. In truth, uncle, the very hour you set out to Court, I eluded the eyes of the Argus placed over me, and fled to the Forest. Is not Robin my betrothed Lord? and as such do I not owe him a duty that supercedes every other. But tell me, what is your business here, disguised thus in person and manners?

Friar. First, answer—How is my daughter? Thank heaven! in the delicacy of her conduct, I may place confidence.

Clorinda. When I parted from my cousin, she was well, but as usual rather melancholy. Now answer me: what is your business here?

Friar. Swear you will not betray me,

Clorinda. On my honour: I would perish first.

Friar. I come here by order of the King, a spy upon your lover.

Clorinda. A spy! O shame, shame! how could you degenerate into so mean an office?

Friar. Remember your promise. His life is in my power: by to-morrow's dawn, the Bishop of Hereford, with five hundred archers, will attack the Forest.

Clorinda. Five hundred archers! a noble force, worthy my Robin's valour. Let come on: with him I'll head his merry-men. cheer his courage, and oppose my bosom to the keenest darts of his enemy. Uncle be assured of this, the woman who would live solely for the man she loves, possesses sufficient courage to die for him.

E 2   *Friar.*

Friar. On your duty grant me one requeſt, and all ſhall be well. Put off your marriage till morning—call up every ſmile and blandiſhment of love and beauty to aid your eloquence—ſolicit, nay, you muſt perſuade your lover to come within his Sovereign's grace. The enemy prepares to invade the land, and his power is neceſſary to his country.

Clorinda. The duty is pleaſing, and I will try my utmoſt.

Friar. His life depends on the event. He comes: ſo remember niece, you muſt defer your nuptials, and you have pledged your honour not to give the moſt diſtant hint of who I am, or of my buſineſs here.

Enter ROBIN, JOHN, *and* RUTTEKIN.

Robin. What, father ſhriving Clorinda; but ſhe has no ſins to anſwer for, except her love for me, and that ſhe has confeſſed in plenitude of goodneſs. Take care, however, ſanctimonious Sir, I ſhall grow jealous, if I catch you thus alone with my love.

Friar. A fig for love; my jug is my love, my wife—My ale my joy, my comfort—A liberal miſtreſs, who, while in my poſſeſſion, ſhall never refuſe to ſhare her favours with my friends.

Robin. Nay, father, you ſhould not conſider drink as a miſtreſs, but a chearful companion to drive away melancholy—ſome wine.—

Friar. Give me ſome wine.

A I R.   (ROBIN HOOD.)

I.

When generous wine expands the ſoul,
How pleaſure hovers round the bowl!
Avaunt ye cares of Fancy's crew,
And give the guilty wretch his due:
But let the juice of ſparkling wine
My groſſer ſenſe of love refine:
As Jove his nectar drinks above,
I'll quaff whole goblets full of love!

Then,

II.

Then why fhou'd I at life repine;
Bring me Venus, bring me wine,
Fill the ever-flowing bowl,
In circles gay and pleasures roll.
Ever open, ever free,
Hail, thou friend to jollity?
My brows with Bachus' chaplets crown'd,
I'll live to love—my cares are drown'd.

Ruttekin. The Friar is moft porterly drunk.

John. True, tinker, and being porterly drunk, he is able to carry his liquor.

Robin. To you, John, I fhall leave the direction of our nuptial fports and paftimes,

John. And I fhall take care to furnifh good amufements. You may expect, lady, fuch archery as Dianna or Apollo could never equal. Then we fhall have at leaft half a dozen heads cracked at quarter-ftaff and fingle-ftick; a few bones broken at foot-ball, and a back or neck fractur'd at wreftling—Oh! we fhall have rare fun!

Clorinda. Not thofe who have their bones broken, John.

John. Then we fhall have bull-baiting and morrice dancing—O how I long to be capering!

Robin. Dance till you fall, John, but no bull-baiting; man has no right to fport with the feelings of thofe creatures which heaven has beftowed for our fuftenance. They die for our ufe, and it is bafe ingratitude to treat them with cruelty.

Clorinda. Thank you for that humane fentiment, my dear Robin.

Robin. Do you go to the young hermit who left us this morning, tell him of my happinefs, and that I requeft his prefence at our feftival. (*To Ruttekin.*

John. Can you find the way, Tinker?

Ruttekin. I paffed the hermitage coming here, and will go forward upon the beaten path: never fear a fool finding his way through the world: fools keep

the

the high road, it is your wife men who go afide and fall into the ditch.

John. You may truft him with the delivery of a meffage; he will be true to your word, though a liar and a tinker.

Ruttckin. No flur upon tinkers; they are found in every honourable profeffion. Your politician's a tinker, in mending the flate-kettle, when he patches up one hole he makes two: your poet's a tinker, he hammers out new works from other mens' old wit; the lawyer's a tinker, he 'deals in brafs and opens more flaws than he ftops; and what's your phyfician? why a tinker too, a brazier of old battered conftitu-. tions, and if he cures you of a gout, will take care to leave a rheumatifm behind for a new job. [*Exit.*

John. Well, I'll to my duty—men, women, and children are bufy in their feveral vocations. The Pindar of Wakefield has brought in a brace of fat bucks, Arthur-a Bland has caught a difh of choice jacks, the maid Marian's preparing the paftry, and tiny Midge the miller is bolting flour for bread—farewel—every one to their vocations; you to amorous dalliance; I to fee pretty Stella twining flowers round the bridle garland. [*Exit.*

Corinda. Poor John's deeply fmitten—Heigh ho! (*Sighs.*)

Robin. That was a figh of grief—Are you not well? Chearly, chearly. Come we will difpute on love, my fweet heart.

Clarinda. On love we muft ever agree: But I would confult with you on your honour—remind you of your own value. Your king has been infulted by an enemy; and will you, my fweet Robin, boafting the blood of Huntingdon and Warwick, endowed with thofe noble qualities, Courage and Generofity, neglect the duty you owe your country, confuming life and reputation within the fequeftered fhades of a foreft.

Robin. You know the wrongs I have fuffered—My fervices overlooked; banifhed on a falfe accufation; ftigmatiz'd with the imputation of a rebellious fpirit;
and

and even you, my betrothed wife, forced from my arms.

Clorinda. Confider, Robin, when our country is in danger, all offences fhould be abfolved; the remembrance of all injuries be forgotten; all parties fhould unite; every heart pant, and every arm act for her honour and defence. Robin, poftpone our nuptials till reconciled to your fovereign; I would marry the leader of an army—not the captain of an outlawed band.

Robin. She fhakes my foul—I will put her heart to the teft (*afide*). I am determined here to fpend my days—here to live as I have done—this you fear—this has fhaken your conftancy.

Clorinda. To doubt my truth is ungenerous. Your fate is mine. But hear me——

Robin. Will you be ever ready, with bended bow, to watch an outlaw and defend his life? Can you fupport the viciffitudes of feafons—endure the fcorching heat and cramping cold? Lodge on the chill ground, and depend for food upon the cafualties of the chace?

Clorinda. All this could I bear, and even more with thee! but hear me—

Robin. Suppofe my affection cooled to thee, and warmed by the beauty of another object—could you with calmnefs fee her fupply your place?

Clorinda. O, Robin! the fight would wound my heart, but not decreafe my love!

Robin. Dearer than life! what, fuffer this for me? Command my pride, my affections—Oh! thou haft foothed my refentments—conquered them—hath roufed my loyalty—thy patriot flame now blazes in my bofom. Yes, Clorinda, I will join my country's arms, and head my merry men. But what has my country to fear? While Englifh-women thus infpire fentiments of public virtue, loyalty, and honour, the number of our enemies will but increafe our victories.

A I R.

A I R.

As burns the charger when he hears
  The trumpet's martial found;
Eager to fcour the field he rears,
  And fpurns th' indented ground;
He fnuffs the air, erects his flowing mane,
Scents the big war, and fweeps along the plain.
  Impatient thus my ardent foul
    Bounds forth on wings of wind,
  And fpurns the moments as they roll
    With lagging pace behind.   *[Exit.*

Clorinda. Poor Robin! I touched him nearly—but he made my heart bleed in return.

Enter ALLEN *and* STELLA.

Stella, well met, I hear terrible complaints of you, child.

Stella. Of me, lady—

Clorinda. Yes, of you, lady. John fays you are cruel, flinty-hearted, and ill-natured.

Allen. And I know he loves her, though too modeft to urge his fuit.

Stella. Loves me! Then indeed he never told me fo; and I rather think he fears me. He approaches me with a cautous ftep, then looks at me with a cunning eye—fo—and when he gives me any thing, if his hand fhould but tonch mine, la, la, he trembles juft as if I was a wild beaft. But I will tell you a-fecret,

Clorinda. A fecret! O mercy, let us hear it.

Stella. I fear I have done a wrong thing. Scarlet has been at our cottage, and he fwore fo much, I promifed to meet him here.

Allen. That was wrong indeed! Never forget, my dear fifter, that to preferve character, we fhould avoid even the appearance of imprudence; a wound on the character of a young female, like an incifion on the bark of a tree, expands with maturity.

Clorinda.

Clorinda. And I have heard that this fame Scarlet, with all his foppery, is an infinuating, defigning fellow; and that more than one unhappy maid mourns his treachery.

Allen. It is true; Lady Martha, one of Stella's faireft companions, is now a wanderer through the Foreft, lamenting and upbraiding, in all the horror of melancholy madnefs, her own weaknefs, and the wickednefs of her feducer. Take example by her, dear Stella,

A I R.

Once fhe was, though now fhe's fad,
As the fpringing feafon glad,
E'er beheld in its domain;
Or fair Summer in her train;
Or rich Autumn in his year:
Sing fhe could as fky-lark clear,
E'er, alas! with grief to tell,
Into ways of fhame fhe fell.
  Now her burthens conftantly,
  " Pity me, maids, pity me;
  " Pity me, a ruin'd maid,
  " Pining in the cyprefs fhade."

Woods that wave o'er mountain tops,
O'er whofe mofs the titmoufe hops,
Tell her tale to ruftling gales;
Fountains weep it through the vales;
And, with her own forrow faint
Sighing Echo joins the plaint.
Martha fair, for ever fad,
Wanders melancholy mad,
  And thus fings fhe bitterly:
  " Pity me, maids, pity me;
  " Pity me, a ruin'd maid,
  " Pining in the cyprefs fhade." [*Exit.*

John. Robin—fair Lady—bleſs me—*(Surprized at ſeeing* STELLA.)

Stella. You ſee I told you truth—He is always frightened at me.

John. I am not frightened—I do not know how it is, but—as I was going to tell you, one of our ſcouts brings word that the biſhop of Hereford has raiſed his men, and is now at Nottingham, with intention to at-tack the foreſt in the morning.

Clorinda I'll to my Robin. John, I have been ſpeak-ing to Stella. She has no diſlike to you. What ſay you, Stella, inſtead of being my bridemaid, will you be a bride yourſelf?

Stella. Heigh ho! my poor heart!

John. Heigh ho! O my poor heart!

Clorinda. Farewel, I leave you together; and, John, take care, make the beſt uſe of your time, you know you have a rival; and this ſame love is a fantaſtical paſſion, a riddle which the wiſeſt cannot reſolve.

A I R.

The flame of love aſſuages
  When once it is reveal'd;
But fiercer ſtill it rages
  The more it is conceal'd.

Conſenting makes it colder,
  When met it will retreat;
Repulſes make it bolder,
  And dangers make it ſweet.

[*Exit.*

John. Hem.

Stella. Heigh ho! Margery.

John. I have ſhot the firſt arrow.　　(*Aſide*)

Stella. Are you there, John?

John. Yes, Stella:——Courage, John, Courage
　　　　　　　　　　　　　　　　(*Aſide.*)
　　　　　　　　　　　　　　　　　Stella.

Stella. Do you fpeak to me, John?

John. There is nobody elfe here, Stella:——I, I, I would——

Stella. La! what would you do?

John. I love you more than——

Stella. More than what?

John. More than the ewe loves her lamb, the doe her fawn, or the dove her mate; I love thee a thoufand times better than I love myfelf.

Stella. And what then?

John. Love me in return.

Stella. And if I fhould, what follows?

John. We fhould do as our parents did before us—marry.

Stella. La! that word marry, is enough to frighten poor little Cupid out of the Foreft: married folks feldom agree—there is George-a-Green abufed his wife in the honey moon, and ftruck her before the end of the year; to be fure fhe has a tongue, and a way of flinging things at his head.——

John. We fhould have none of this work, Stella; though fuch domeftic breezes are as neceffary in fome families as thunder ftorms in hot weather; the one clears the houfe of foul language, and the other frees the air of foul vapours.

Stella. Then, John, my brother fays I am too young; though I want only eleven months, one week and two days of eighteen. But how fhould we maintain ourfelves?

John. Prudent foul; how fhe looks forward to a young family!—I will maintain you by my wit, my girl; a means by which many great folks hold up their heads; befides, I have goods and chattels, all the furniture you have feen in my cottage fhall be yours; and egad I will throw all you have not feen into the bargain.

Stella. Thank you from my heart, John—and in return, all I poffefs is at your fervice.

John.

John. Honeftly fpoken; fo thus I fieze upon the fruits of your father's induftry, and your mother's labour. *(Kiffes her.*

Friar. (*Within*) This way—this way—

Stella. Mercy! here are fome men coming.

John. Who in the name of Old Nick are they? Let us ftand fide and fee.

Enter FRIAR, SCARLET, *and two* ARCHERS.

Friar. See, gentlemen, the bifhop of Hereford will not come alone; the King's forces join him, and you can have no chance from oppofition; fo convey me to Nottingham, and I'll infure pardon to every man who accompanies me.

Scarlet. What fay you, lads?

1ft. Archer. We will follow the fortunes of our Captain.

2d. Archer. But can we in confcience defert our Captain.

Friar. No more about confcience.—But come, I'll put it to the trial, and here is the ordeal, (*takes out a purfe*); here is the general abfolution that falves our confciences.—This opens and fhuts the mouths of the moft vociferous orators, blinds the eyes of the church, deafens the ears of magiftrates, obliterates the judgment of the law, arrefts the arm of juftice, and dries up the fountains of mercy. How feels your confcience now?

Archer. It tells me I am in duty bound to obey my fpiritual paftor.

Friar, Religioufly fpoken. Here, take the fuller's earth that removes all ftains. [*Gives money.*

Scarlet. Friar, I want no money; my terms are thefe: This night I keep watch with my friends; now, when our company is afleep, we will feize upon Stella, carry her off, and thus reward myfelf.

John. I'll take care of that, you treacherous rafcal. Here's for you, fanctified devil (*Knocks down the Friar with his pole, then draws his fword*; Scarlet *alfo draws:*
- *the*

the Archers *run off.)* And now for you, good Mafter
Scarlet, whom I fhall in a few minutes cafe—clofe as a
hare—Yes, I'll fkin and carbonade you, you dog.

Scarlet. Come on.——

Stella. (*Runs between them.*) Help! Murder!
Help!

Enter ALLEN *and* ARCHERS; *they feize* SCARLET *and the*
FRIAR. STELLA *runs to* JOHN.

John. Is this the return for the hofpitable reception
our Captain gave you?   [*To the* Friar.

Friar. Bring me before your Captain, that is all I
defire.

John. As for you, rafcal, you fhall die like a traitor.
[*To* Scarlet.

Allen. Say, what is the matter?

John. This hypocritical Friar I have difcovered in
the very act of bribing our men to defert with him to
Nottingham, for the purpofe of betraying us; and
Scarlet here was to carry off your fifter Stella.

Allen. We will not difturb brave Robin with them
now. Let them be confined clofe prifoners till morning.

Friar. I fubmit, but do not ufe me ill; for remember, no man ever injured the church with impunity.
[*Exit* Friar *and* Scarlet, *guarded.*

Allen. It was luck'ly, John, that you were fo near.

Stella. It was indeed. He once faved my life, and
now preferved my honour.

Allen. Which entitles him to your heart. (*Horns*)
But, hark! the merry Archers are returning from the
evening's chace.

Enter ARCHERS *defcending from winding hills at the
further part of the Stage.*

GLEE.

Hark! the leafy woods refounding
  Echo to the bugle-horn;
Swift the ftag with vigor bounding,
  Leaps the break, and clears the thorn.

Ev'ry

Ev'ry heart his cunning trying,
  Shafts arreſt his eager flight ;
High he leaps, the hounds full crying,
  Now he's vaniſh'd from our ſight.

Twanging bows with death purſuing,
  Now he rears and turns his head,
Bays the dogs ; but nought from ruin,
  Nought can ſave—he falls—he's dead !

Sound the horn, huzza in chorus,
  We are free from care, my boys ;
Rural pleaſures lie before us,
  Health, and length, and ſtrength of joys.

A C T   III.

SCENE, *a deep view of the Foreſt ; dark ;* RUTTEKI
diſcovered ſitting croſs-legg'd.

RUTTEKIN.

SO, after all my boaſting, I have loſt my way ; but
that is common with men of genius, and women
of genius too. There is your great orator ; he often
leaves the plain road of truth, to wander in the laby-
rinth of falſhood. Then your prude, perhaps, after
walking years in the ſtraight paths of virtue, trips in
her gait, and, ſtumbling, falls upon a bed of thorns.
" Few people purſue the tract Nature deſigned them—
" therefore we find politicians without brains, magi-
" ſtrates without juſtice, noblemen without honour,
" traders without honeſty, philoſophers without mo-
" rality, and churchmen without religion.."——
  Annette. (Within.) Hilloa ! hilloa !
  Ruttek. Here comes ſome ſhepherd's boy, bleating
like one of his lambs.

                  Enter

Enter ANNETTE.

Annette. Mercy! how dark!

Ruttek. Hilloa!—

Annette. Heaven preferve me!——Pity me, if you are a human creature.

Ruttek. I am a human creature, but with an appetite keen as a wolf.

Annette. Sure you are the tinker I met this morning!

Ruttek. Right, my little popping-jay; but where is your companion?

Annette. I have loft him in the Foreft; help me to feek him, and he fhall reward you liberally.

Ruttek. Reward me! give me your hand—Reward me!—I have been out, I find, in my road, but not in my reckoning.   [*Exeunt.*

Enter ANGELINA.

A I R.

The morn, who night adorning,
    In filver veftments bound,
Retires, that ruddy morning
    May breathe her fweets around.
Edwin thus beguiling,
With eyes illum'd and fmiling,
    Soft maidens' hearts del'ghting,
        Ev'ry foul cou'd move;
But I this treafure flighting,
    In darknefs feek my love!

Enter RUTTEKIN *and* ANNETTE *at a diftance.*

Annette. It is my mafter's voice.——Speak, Sir, I am here.

Ruttek. Yes, your man is here, pleafe your honour, and him with a tinker, who brought him to you—but not for the fake of the reward he promifed.

Angelina I am fatigued with wandering through this Foreft, fo dark and dreary.

                                    Rutek.

Rut ek. It is a fashionable situation, your honour; most of our great folks are bewildered, or in the dark.

Angelina. Do you live in the Foreft, Sir?

Ruttek. No; I ftarve in the Foreft, Sir.

Annette. Are there any inhabitants to be found here, Mafter Tinker?

Ruttek. Yes, bucks and does in plenty; as many horned cattle as any city can boaft. I am now in fearch of a hermit, with an invitation to Robin Hood's wedding, which is to be celebrated in the morning.

Annette. Your coufin Clorinda, you hear, has not ftood upon punctilio.

Angelina. Well, Sir, permit us to accompany you in fearch of this fame hermit.——I am very weak, *(leans on* Annette*)* but feel moft for you, my faithful companion; for myfelf no mifery is too great. *[Nightingale fings.)*

Annette. Hark! I hear the harbinger of love! A happy omen!

Angelina. It is indeed the nightingale!

Ruttek. Yes, and prefently you will hear the fcreech-owl. *(Bell tolls.)*

Annette. There goes the curfew of fome neighbouring town; the found comes from the left.—Tinker, lead on.

Angelina. O my ruined love!

Annette. You did not ruin him, he was very poor!

Angelina. Peace: He was rich in virtues; wealth nor power were not his, it is true; but he had wifdom, truth, and generofity—thofe fhould have been all to me.

Ruttek. Come, gentlefolks, I wait.

Annette. We come, tinker.—Pray do not weep.

[To Angelina.

Angelina. Yes, weep for ever, though in vain. Not all the dew of heaven can revive the cropped violet.

Ruttek. Pr'ythee, mend your pace; this wood is haunted by the ghofts of gibbeted thieves, and murdered travellers.—Blefs me! I heard a noife—no; it was the wind. Robin Goodfellow and his brother fai-
ries

ries have been often feen here !—Lift ! I hear a ruftling in the bufhes—fome cut-throat, no doubt.

Annette. Why tremble fo?   [*Holding him*

Ruttek. I tremble, thou aguifh afpin ! (*Shaking.*)— Sir, do you not hear the devil, or fome evil fpirit ?
     [*To* Angelina.

Annette. Some one approaches—and fee yonder a glimmering light fparkles in the dark, perhaps in fome cottage window.

Ruttek. Yes, and it moves this way, houfe and all.

EDWIN *appears at the upper end of the Stage with a Lantern.*

Angelina. Heaven preferve us !

Ruttek. And forgive us our fins.—O my poor confcience ! The poultry I have ftolen are pecking at it, and the lambs baaing in my ears.

Annette. Silence, coward !

Ruttek. I am dumb.—But who ever looked on the devil without quaking ?—No, it is not the devil, but a ghoft or hobgoblin.—Nay, it is the devil too, for I his great faucer eyes blazing with blue fire !

Angelina. Peace, coward ! perhaps fome benighted traveller, like ourfelves.

Ruttek. It is the devil, I fay; look at his cloven feet, great horns, and monftrous noftrils !——I'll to prayers.——   [*Kneels,*

Edwin. O my heart !——

Ruttek. It is a broken hearted poor devil too.

Annette. Indeed that was a bitter figh.

Angelina. I felt it in my bofom.

Edwin. How dark and ftill the night !—how fuited to the fituation of my foul ! Oh Love, Love ! why prefent her image to my mind, whofe chilling breath froze my fond youthful hopes, and funk me to defpair ?

G   BAL-

BALLAD.

Since all my hopes, dear maid,
 Are blown to air,
And my fond heart's betrayed
 To sad despair;
Here in this wildernefs
My forrows I'll rehearfe,
And thy hard-heartednefs,
 Thou cruel fair.

" Wild fruits fhall be my meat;
 " I'll drink the fpring;
" Cold earth fhall be my feat;
 " For covering
" I'll have the ftarry fky
" My head to canopy,
" Until my foul on high
 " Doth take her wing."

No bell, no fun'ral fire,
 No tears for me;
No grave do I defire,
 Nor obfequy.
The gentle red-breaft, he
With leaves will cover me,
And fing my elegy
 Moft dolefully.

Ruttek. You may fing, Oh be joyful! this certainly
is the Hermit.   [*Goes toward* Edwin.

Edwin. Stand off.—Who are you?

Ruttek. Zounds! it is not the Hermit!

Edwin. Speak, I fay; you have no injury to fear
from me.

Annette. We are two young Pilgrims, who have loft
our way, and wander in the horrors of the Foreft.

Ruttek. And a poor Tinker, almoft famifhed to
death.

         Angelena.

Angelina. Who calls upon your compaſſion to guide their wearied ſteps to ſome hoſpitable cottage!

Edwin. Your voice breathes gentleneſs—your hand young man.——The day already breaks—my cell is near, where you may reſt in ſafety : ſimple fare, and a couch of ruſhes, are at your ſervice.

Ruttek. Poor ſouls! the lantern you carry in your poop frightened them out of their wits ; they took you one time for a ghoſt ; then for a hobgoblin ; then for a Will-o'-th'-Wiſp ; and at laſt, for the Devil himſelf! Heaven bleſs us! though I did all I could to encourage them, I ſhall never forget how they ſhook.

Annette. Nor I how you confeſſed ſtealing the poultry and lambs.

Edwin. Come on, I'll lead the way, and if free from that tyrant paſſion, Love, my habitation may enſure you a comfortable repoſe.

Angelina. Oh, my heart!

Edwin. Grief I perceive ſits heavy on your mind, and weighs your ſpirits down ; you mourn a broken fortune, a falſe friendſhip, or a deſerted love.

Angelina. Gentle hermit, broken fortune, nor falſe friendſhip are not the cauſes of my melancholy.

[*Exeunt* Edwin *and* Angelina.

Ruttekin. No, we mourn empty bellies, my ribs ſtick as cloſe together as the two ſhells of an oyſter. Come, out with your purſe, youngſter : the reward, the reward.

Annette. Reward! a ſound beating is the proper reward for a coward ; beſides, thou art a liar for denying thy cowardice, and a rogue for demanding what you have no right to.

Ruttekin. The very reaſons why I ſhould have my reward ; you ſee my garments are as ſeedy as a gingerbread cake ; out at the elbows like a poet ; ſo ſince I am a rogue and a liar, and ragged withal, give me the money lad, that I may get out of my bad *habits*.

Annette. Here, ſirrah : (*gives money.*) This can procure you every thing but that you want moſt, *honeſty.*

Ruttek.

Rutteken. Never mind that : heaven bleſs him who makes me a rich rogue. O that I was now in Robin Hood's bower; it is there where plenty reigns, and good cheer keeps revel, and by this time the bridal breakfaſt is preparing.

A I R.

Gently burns the greenwood fire;
  Lay the veniſon down to roaſt ;
Dreſs it quickly I deſire,
  In the dripping put a toaſt :
Hark ! I hear the jack go round ;
O the veniſon's nicely brown'd !

Green-geeſe, ducklings, juicy meat ;
  Capon, widgeon, partridge, quail ;
Pies, tarts, dumplings, puddings ſweet ;
  Peas and beans, and butter'd kale ;
Spices hunger to create ;
O ye Gods ! how I ſhould eat !

On the table dinner lies,
  See the charming white and red ;
Cut it up, the gravy flies,
  On the ſweeteſt graſs it fed.
Hark ! I hear the jack go round ;
Oh the veniſon's nicely brown'd !

See they ſpread the lilly cloth,
  Knives are ſharp and forks are clean ;
Pickles criſp, and ſallads both,
  Now appear ſo freſh and green ;
With ſtrong beer, old ale and wine,
O, ye Gods ! how I ſhould dine !   [*Exit.*

SCENE, *Outſide of the Huts.* Enter JOHN, BOWMAN
and ARCHERS.

Bowman. Well John, his reverence the Biſhop of Hereford has not ventured to attack us.

John.

John. No: he waits the return of our prisoner, the Curtle Friar, who I am convinced is his spy; but Robin will truss him up, " and he is right, I have no notion of spiritual pastors laying aside the keys of Saint Peter, to take up the sword of Saint Paul."

Bowman. Right, John.——

John. But let me tell you, all our cares are at an end: Clorinda has persuaded Robin to make proper concessions to the King, and join him in drubbing the enemy. He will be Earl of Huntingdon again: I'll be a Knight, Stella a Lady, and you a 'Squire; but this is losing time. Let the prisoners be brought forward: (*Exit an Archer*) we will first dispatch them, and then all get as mad as so many March hares.

Enter ARCHER, *carrying a large Gothic Chair*: *Archers.*

John. Fix the bench of justice here, which is made of Yew, signifying the bitterness of judgment, We should have tried this wicked priest and our treacherous companion before day, but judicial proceedings ought never to be carried on in the dark.

Bowman. Nor in twilight, John; therefore we English hate Star-chamber business. But it is now broad light, shall we proceed?

John. Yes: but first bring me in the robes and coif, we stripped from the learned Serjeant of the law, on his way to the parvise. (*Exit Archer.*) A judge might as well appear without his head as without his robe; for professional wisdom consists much in looking grave.

Enter ARCHER *with Robe and Coif.*

John. (*Puts on the robes.*) Great knowledge and *pocus pocus* lie deposited under this coif. Now I am equipt in the uniform of the courts, and qualified to hear and determine causes. (*Sits.*) Do I look wise?——

Bowman. Aye, as wise as an owl at midnight—So wise, were you to appear in Westminster-hall, on a call of Serjeants, the judges might cry out, " I spy a brother!"

John.

John. Order in the prifoners and witneffes.—Though
to be fure I am acquainted with the whole cafe myfelf;
but then, being a judge, I muſt know nothing but
what comes out in evidence.

Bowman. Shall we impannel a jury?

John. A jury! Piſh, no: where is the neceffity?
Juries follow the direction of the court: yet we may as
well have one for form's fake. Range yourfelves Archers for the jury. (*The Archers range themfelves in a
row.*) Now bring in the profecutors and the profe-
cutees.

Enter FRIAR *and* SCARLET, *bound.*

John. Why are the prifoners bound? For ſhame,
Bowman! A man upon his trial ſhould be perfectly at
eafe in his body, that he may have the free ufe of his
mind. (*The prifoners are unbound.*) Now carry away
the ropes: the fight of the halters may be offenfive, or
raife a fellow-feeling, and difturb fome of the jury.
Command filence.

Bowman. Silence!

John. You father Tuck, and you William Scarlet,
ſtand charged with carrying on a correfpondence with
the Biſhop of Hereford, and an intention to betray us,
Lords and Yeomen of the Foreft, into his hands.

Bowman. How fay you, William Scarlet; guilty or
not guilty.

Scarlet. Not guilty.

John. Not guilty! Say fo again, you damned dog.
and you ſhall be hanged without further trial, as a notorious liar.—Will you challenge any of the jury?

Scarlet. You know, John, I'd fight the beft of them.

John. Fight the beft of you: he don't underftand
the term; but, gentlemen, it is legal practice that the
prifoner ſhould be ignorant of the proceedings carried
on againft him.   (*To the Archers.*)

Scarlet. Will you liften to reafon?

John. Liften to reafon! No, firrah, not on the part
of the prifoner: I fit here as a judge of law, not of
reafon :

reafon; befides, I have four reafons for hanging you. 'Firft, you muft be hanged, becaufe I am not to fit here for nothing: fecondly, you muft be hanged, becaufe you have nobody to ftand up for you: thirdly, you muft be hanged, becaufe you appear in *forma pauperis* without money ; and, fourthly, you muft be hanged, becaufe you have a damned hanging look. Gentlemen, I have finifhed my charge.

Bowman. Gentlemen of the jury, are you agreed? Is the prifoner guilty, or not guilty ?

Archer. Guilty.

Bowman. Put him bye. Stand forward, Friar. Friar Tuck, are you guilty or not guilty?

Friar. Guilty.

John. The firft truth I believe you ever told.

Friar. May I fpeak.

John. Not after conviction—Take him away,

(*The Archers feize him*

Friar. One word——

John. Stop his mouth.—

Friar. I plead my clergy.

John. Plead your clergy !—The devil you do?—Oh, ho !——Gentlemen of the Jury, this is point of law, and muft be left to Robin Hood. I fhall only obferve, that it is really a ftrange doctrine, that men of the church and men of letters, fhould commit with impu- nity crimes for which other men fuffer without mercy.

Enter Robin, Clorinda, *and* Stella.

Robin. John you are early at duty.

John. Yes, Juftice fhould never fleep.

Robin. True, John, nor fhould Mercy ever clofe her eyes.

Clorinda. That fentiment breathes philanthropy. How this, uncle ? I have perfuaded my Robin to fue his So- vereign for grace. (*Afide.*)

Friar. Then procure my difmiffion, and all is well. (*Afide.*)

Clorinda. May I interfere ?——

John.

John. The bufinefs is over, madam, we have fully convicted the prifoners : will you pronounce judgment on the Friar? *(To* Robin.) Shall we hang him up, or cut him down?

Robin. We will leave him, John, to the accufations of his own confcience; a feverer punifhment than any we can inflict. Your profeffion, Sir, fhould have taught you principles of honour.

John. Principles of honour!—You miftake your man : this fellow is one of thofe itinerant mendicants who travel the country, and ripen in the funfhine of public charity, producing very little devotion, with a plentiful crop of fenfuality.

Friar. Will you difmifs me?

John. Yes, to the other world.

Robin. Prudence will juftify my inflicting on you the fevereft punifhment; but humanity forbids it. Go to the proud bifhop of Hereford, and tell him, an outlaw inftructed a church-man, by example, that charity which he fhould practice as well as teach.

Friar. I obey; and your meffage fhall be delivered literally. But be affured, when next we meet, you fhall not have all the advantage; I will have ample fatisfaction for this generofity.

Robin. Bowman, order him fafe conduct through the Foreft.——*(Exeunt* Friar and *Bowman.)*——And now for you, Sir, *(To* Scarlet) your ingratitude hurts me, and your bafe intent upon this innocent girl I cannot forgive: " for, let me tell you, Sir, there does not " exift a greater wretch than he, who, by perfuafion " and perjury, feduce to fhame the object of his " paffion."

John. " I know of none greater, except the villain, " who, having ruined, abandons."

Stella. Might I implore his pardon, on condition——

Robin. What is the condition, Stella?

Stella. That he marries poor Martha, She is juft now returned to her mother's cottage, overwhelmed with grief.

Robin

Robin. This, if he performs, fhall again reftore him to the Foreft——(*Exit* Scarlet.)——Come, girls, the morming is fine, and wefhall roufe a ftag before break-faft.

Stella. " You'll excufe me; I never found pleafure in worrying animals innocent as they are beautiful; and who have neither cunning to avoid nor courage to face their purfuers." [*Exit.*

Clorinda. Robin, lead on; I'll accompany you and your merry archers to the chace.

A   I   R.

When ruddy Aurora awakens the day,
And bright dew-drops impearl the flow'rs fo gay
Sound, found, my ftout archers! found horns and
  away,
 With arrows fharp pointed we go.
See Sol now appearing in fplendor fo bright,
IO PÆAN! for Phœbus, who leads to delight,
All glorious in beauty he rifes to fight;
 'Tis he, boys, is God of the bow.

Sweet rofes we'll offer at Venus's fhrine,
Libations we'll pour to Bacchus' divine,
While mirth, love, and pleafure, in junction combine,
 For archers, true fons of the game!
Bid forrow, adieu! in foft numbers we'll fing
Love, friendfhip, and beauty, fhall make the air ring,
Wifhing health and fuccefs to our country and King.
 Encreafe to their honour and fame. [*Exeunt.*

SCENE, *the infide of* EDWIN'S *cave; a ruftic altar with a wooden crofs, and a death's-head.* RUITEKIN *fleeping on a trufs of rufhes:* ANGELINA *and* ANNETTE *fitting at a table.*

Angelina. Here fhould I wifh to take up my abode, and like the benevolent hermit of this cell, exhauft my days in prayers and repentance. (*Rifes.*

Annette. He fometimes fighs as bitterly as yourfelf.

      Angelina.

Angelina. Oh, there is no grief like mine! Reflect on the man I loved!—Not the sweets of opening blosom, refined by the dew of heaven, could emulate the purity of his mind.—The dew, the blosom, the sweets were his! but woe to me! the inconstancy of their charms was mine.

Enter EDWIN.

Edwin. Hail, my youthful guests! I hope this humble cell has afforded you comfort?

Angelina. We owe you grateful thanks.

Edwin. The morning sun has pierced the Forest's gloom, and glitters on the dew; the feather'd choristers chaunt their mattins to that bounteous power which gave them being; and nature seems alive to love and chearfulnefs; while man, ungrateful man alone! overlooks thofe bleffings which the all-wife, the all-benignant hand of Heaven daily pours on him.   [*Walks to* RUTTEKIN.

Angelina. What perfuafive melody breathes in his voice!

Annette. I could hear him preach for an hour. Pity fo fenfible, fo young and clever a man fhould turn Hermit.

Edwin. See where this fool, improvident of time, fhrouded in temporary death, dozes through life, and indolently lofes Heaven's moft precious gifts, the exercife of thought and reafon. Awake! awake, fluggard! the morning wears apace.

Ruttek. Why difturb me?—Yet, by my apetite it is time to rife.

Edwin. Young Pilgrim, my heart participates the grief that evidently afflicts you, and my foul vibrates with thofe involuntary fighs you in vain attempt to fupprefs. Tell me whence flow your forrows. (*Takes* Angelina *by the hand.*) This foft hand has not long grafped a pilgrim's ftaff.

Angelina. Oh, my love-worn heart!

Edwin. Is love the bane that cankers thy young breaft? Haplefs youth! Some proud, fome faithlefs woman has deftroyed your peace.

Angelina.

Angelina. Forgive the rudeneſs of a ſtranger, whoſe unhallowed feet intrudes where Heaven and you re-ſide.

Edwin. Let me know your ſtory.—Beſhrew his heart who injured you! By Heaven I pity, and would re-dreſs your wrongs.

Angelina. You feel too much for me. I have been cruel, ungrateful.—Methinks I could confide in you. —Let us retire, and, as you wiſh to know my ſtory, I will unboſom my heart to you in full confeſſion, and follow your advice.

A I R.

Bright Sol now darts on yielding night
His beams of orient light;
He ſpeeds his fiery race
O'er fields of azure ſpace,
Whilſt I am wretched and forlorn,
He ſtill returns to bleſs the morn!
Once, ah! once I roſe, free as the ſun,
Each day ſmiling gay and bright,
  Life elating,
  Joy creating,
Smiling peace and ſoft delight
Crown'd the day, and bleſs'd the night.

[*Exeunt* Angelina *and* Edwin.

Ruttek. Tell me, youngſter, what crime has this maſter of yours committed? Something terrible, for hisconſcience is moſt horribly haunted.

Annette. But not with the ghoſts of poultry or young lambs, maſter Tinker.

Ruttek. No more of that, if you love me——But ſay, where are you come from?

Annette. We, as you may perceive by this badge, fought in the holy wars.

Ruttek. That was pious; you cut the throats of the Pagans for the honour of Heaven, and the good of your own ſouls.

Annette

Annette. In one engagement my mafter fplit a Vizier to the chine, and I cut down a Bafhaw of three tails.

Ruttek. Ha! ha! He was devil of a Bafhaw!—— And you cut off his tails!

Annette. True; but it being our misfortune to be taken prifoners, we were carried to the houfe of a Mufti, where my mafter falling in love with the Mufti's wife, and being difcovered by him in the lady's apartment, to fave himfelf, he ftabbed the old fellow to the heart.'

Ruttek. That was right; it was ferving Heaven to kill a Turk.

Annette. We fled of courfe; and, after long wandering, came to a fea-port, where we took fhipping, and at laft arrived in Old England.

Ruttek. And pray now, had you any love-affair upon your hands?

Annette—Certainly—I intrigued in the feraglio of a Janiffary, who had a wife for every week, and a concubine for every day in the year.

Ruttek. O, poor fellow! he had an almanack full of them. But I cannot help laughing at a fellow with fuch a pigmy perfon and fqueak-pipe voice getting among fo many women.

Annette. Why, firrah, wherever I travel, hundreds folicit my favours; but I am cruel, except to one maid only. `

A I R.

My name is little Harry-O,
Mary I will marry-O
In fpite of Nell, or Ifabel,
I'll follow my own vagary-O.
   With my rigdum jigdum airy-O,
   I love little Mary-O,
     In fpite of Nell,
     Or Ifabel,
   I'll follow my own vagary-O.
Smart fhe is and bonny-O,
Sweet as fugar candy-O;

Frefh

Fresh and gay,
    As flow'rs in May,
And I'm her Jack-a-dandy-O.
    With my, &c.
Soon to church I'll have her-O,
Where we'll wed together-O;
    And that, that done,
    Then we'll have fun,
In spite of wind and weather-O.
    With my rigdum jigdum airy-O,
    I love little Mary-O;
        In spite of Nell,
        Or Isabel,
    I'll follow my own vagary-O.

Enter EDWIN *and* ANGELINA *from the cave.*

Edwin. And is it—O Heaven!—Is it my love, my Angelina!————

Angelina. I am your love indeed.   [*They embrace.*

Ruttek. That is natural; after high words, they fall to wrestling.

Annette. Yes, and the hermit will probably get the better of the pilgrim.

Angelina. Annette, Annette, I have found my love, my Edwin!——Oh, that I should not know thee?—But three years absence, grief, and the hermit's habit, have caused the change. I have felt, for three long years, my spirit pine through weeping hours; but now thy smile lights up my mind, and all my sorrows vanish like a fleeting dream.

Edwin. Thou art altered too; the rose of beauty is opened into bloom.—Here I could gaze, and feast my eyes for ever!——

Ruttek. But, Sir, we cannot all partake of that breakfast; so let us have something more solid.

Annette. Peace, idiot!——Sir, I wish you happiness: this meeting has saved us a long journey; we were on our way to the Holy Land.

Angelina.

A'gelina. We were indeed! I had refolved to find thee, Edwin, or perifh in the attempt.

Edwin. Let us to the merry archers.—The brave Earl of Huntingdon is my friend, and will fhare my felicity.

D U E T.

EDWIN.

Thus let me hold thee to my heart,
  And every care refign.

ANGELINA.

And fhall we never, never part,
  My life, my all that's mine!

BOTH.

No; never from this hour to part,
  We'll live and love fo true,
The figh that rends the conftant heart,
  Shall break thy Edwin's too; }
  Breaks Angelina's too. }

             [*Exeunt* Angelina *and* Edwin.

Ruttek. So you are a woman, he, he, he: what a confounded fool have I been not to difcover it fooner —Then, O mercy! what a legion of lies you have been telling about the Bafhaw, the Mufti, the Grand Vizier, the Janniffary, their wives, their concubines, and their tails——What think you of me?

Annette. Tolerable enough, as a tinker; but moft abominably as a man.—

Ruttekin. They are going to—to—to—marry.

Annette. What then?

Ruttek. I have a great mind to pop the queftion to her—So I will—No, I wont (*afide*)—Tell me, thou filver fkinned lafs with the golden locks, will you?—

Annette. What?

Ruttek. Nothing—Yes—but I'll tell you as we trip along will—Never faw a girl better made for carrying a tinker's budget.—But come, now for the marriage feftival.

                        A I R

A I R.

We'll to the bow'r of Robin Hood,
   This is the wedding day;
And merrily in blithe Sherwood,
   Bridefmaids and bridefmen play.
      Then follow me, my bonny lafs
      And we'll the paftimes fee;
      For the minftrels fing,
      And the fweet bells ring,
      And they feaft right merrily, merrily.

The humming beer flows round in pai's,
   With mead that's ftout and old;
And am'rous virgins tell love tales,
   To thaw the heart that's cold.
      Then follow, me, &c.

There dancing fprightly on the green,
   Each light-foot lad and lafs;
Sly ftealing kiffes when unfeen,
   And jingling glafs with glafs.
      Then follow me, &c.   [*Exeunt.*

SCENE *changes to the outfide of* ROBIN HOOD's *bower.*
   Enter JOHN, SCARLET, *and* STELLA.

Scarlet. Allen, your forgivenefs makes me your
friend for ever; and believe, me, John, you have my
warmeft thanks: in protecting female innocence, you
only performed a duty incumbent on every man. But
how can I ever expiate the injury I intended you, fair
Stella?

Stella. Your promife of marriage to poor weeping
Martha, proves your repentance; and I not only forgive, but will, as far as poffible, forget your tranf-
greffion.

Scarlet. Then I am fatisfied.—From this day, Martha fhall find me kind and conftant, and in promoting
her happinefs, I'll fecure my own.

Stella Your converfation makes us all happy, as far
as it is poffible for us to be fo.

A I R.

A I R.

Hark! the warbling choir fings,
Hark! the azure welkin rings,
 Hills with joy refound;
Cowflips glad the laughing fields,
Fragrant thyme its odour yields,
 Violets breathe around.

Elms their verdant honour fpread,
Dew-drops gild the moffy bed,
 Daifies bloom among;
Soft and joyous through the fkies,
Thoufand fprightly voices rife,
 Echo joins the fong.

Blifsfull fcenes foon pafs away,
Pride's the glimmer of a day,
 Flies on rapid wing;
Learn to know, vain mortal man,
Fleeting life is but a fpan,
 Emblem of the fpring.

Enter RUTTEKIN

Ruttekin. Save you, gentle folks.——Here am I re-
turned with my ftomach hollow as an empty fauce-pan.
The hermit is arrived, and with him two ftrangers.
Where is madam Clorinda? where is bold Robin?
Here is a fine Lord, with a brave train, juft alighted
——Lord a' mercy on us!—Where are all the Archers?
Where is John, Scarlet, &c?—Here, here—this way,
this way.   [*All hurry off.*

Flourifh. The SCENE *draws, and difcovers the infide of*
ROBIN'S *bower; the* FRIAR *dreffed as Baron* FITZ-
HERBERT, CLORINDA, ANGELINA, STELLA, ALLEN,
ANNETTE, &c.

Clorinda. My dear uncle, you have performed your
promife nobly.

            Fitz-

Pitzherbert. I am no longer a tipling curtel Friar but Baron Fitzherbert; and behold my credentials. (*Takes out a parchment.*)—His Majefty's free pardon to all within the Foreft.

John. Mercy! What virtue lies in a piece of parchment with a bit of wax to it!

Fitz. Your humanity and benevolence have obliterated from the royal breaft every remembrance of refentment. I have it in command to inveft you with your former dignities, honours, manors, and caftles; and now falute you Robert Earl of Huntingdon.

John. Now I like this——But what preferment, place, or penfion, have you got for me?

Fitz. As you are a judge, John, chufe for yourfelf —Will you be hanged up or cut down?—Nay, no anfwer after conviction, or I fhall produce four reafons.

John. A fig for your reafons!—Here is my fugar plumb.   [*Takes* Stella *by the hand.*

Fitz. Clorinda, I beftow you on Robin with all my heart; and to you, my daughter, I prefent your faithful lover.—And may beauty and virtue ever reward conftancy.

Robin. The royal bounty overpowers me, and your goodnefs foftens my heart, even to infant tendernefs. This day we dedicate to love.—To-morrow I will reaffume my ftation, and, in the fervice of my King and Country lead my merry archers to victory.

F I N A L E.

SCARLET *and* STELLA.

Let the mufic fprightly play,
This is Hymen's holida ;
Smiling virtues him await,
Guardian of the married ftate.
   CHORUS. Let the mufic, &c.

Rofeat God of foft defire,
Mirth and wit, and fong infpire:
Each fond heart elate with joy,
Honeft love can never cloy.
   CHORUS. Let the, &c.

I

ANGELINA

ANGELINA *and* EDWIN.

Dimpled Innocence appear,
Free from forrow, void of fear;
Tny fair fifter bring with thee,
Captivating Modefty.
                    CHORUS. Let the, &c.

C A T C H.

FRIAR, RUTTEKIN, *and* JOHN.

Fill the foaming horn up high,
Nor let tuneful lips be dry;
Let the b. iming goblet fmile,
Blood-red v ine our cares beguile.

ROBIN *and* CLORINDA.

Strains of liberty we'll fing,
To our C untry, Queen, and King,
To thofe friends, who fien here
With their fmiles our bofoms cheer.
                    CHORUS, Strains of &c.

F I N I S.

www.ingramcontent.com/pod-product-compliance
Lightning Source LLC
Chambersburg PA
CBHW031747090426
42739CB00008B/918